Memoirs of the
Automotive Aftermarket

BY RON TODD

DORRANCE
PUBLISHING CO
EST. 1920
PITTSBURGH, PENNSYLVANIA 15238

Dorrance Publishing Co
585 Alpha Drive
Pittsburgh, PA 15238
Visit our website at *www.dorrancebookstore.com*

ISBN: 979-8-88683-484-0
eISBN: 979-8-88683-572-4

Memoirs of the Automotive Aftermarket

THIS WRITING IS AN ACCOUNT OF WHERE WE STARTED, where we are and where we could be heading in the automotive aftermarket business. The writer has vast experience in automotive aftermarket auto parts and auto repair facilities. While we look at where we came from, there will be some history that will explain America's fascination with the automobile. Created as simple transportation, we have taken the automobile to new heights with every generation. Americans have taken this simple concept of transportation and have made it to be the second largest expenditure per household for most families. Being in the automotive aftermarket business, we have needed to evolve with automobile owners' love, expectations and need for their vehicles. We have learned we cannot treat automobiles and owners as we have in the past. The learning process has changed with every generation and there are aftermarket parts and repair companies that have not survived due to their unwillingness to change while there are some that are strong today because of their willingness to change. As you will see from the writings, real life experience has taught me why listening to the customer has always and remains to be the most important process in staying "with the times". While listening is important, action must follow. Automobile owners have a love for style, color, performance, and longevity for their vehicles. We must learn each customer has needs and respond to them accordingly. Today, information is easier to gather than it was in any time in history. The World Wide Web has made shoppers smarter and more informed than ever before. This is something auto parts stores and repair shops can capitalize on if they choose. The intent of this writing is to help the automotive aftermarket understand their customer. The writer has experience in owning and operating auto parts stores and automotive repair facilities. Change is constant in this industry and will continue to be with improvements coming with each new year.

One of the greatest generals in military history was Napoleon Bonaparte. Made a full general at age twenty-six, he utilized shrewd strategy, bold cunning, and lightning speed to his advantage to win many victories. The Duke of Wellington, one of the general's most formidable enemies, said, "I consider Napoleon's presence in the field to equal forty thousand men in the balance."

"I will tell you the mistake you are always making," Napoleon said addressing an opponent he had defeated. "You draw up your plans the day before battle, when you do not yet know your adversary's movements." Napoleon recognized in his losing opponent a weakness that he himself did not have: Lack of adaptability. If you are willing to change and adapt for the sake of your team, you always have a chance to win.

PREFACE

HOW DID THIS ALL START?

I am quite interested in history and grew up watching western (cowboy) movies. Every cowboy or cowgirl had a special horse and in many cases, we would learn the horse's name as well as the main character of the movie. This seemed to make the experience of the movie personal. I felt I knew the characters in the movies and their horses so much that after the movie, we children would gather outside and act out the movies for ourselves. We did not have fancy guns you bought at the store that made firing sounds; we picked up a stick and broke small branches to form the shape of a gun. I have wiped out many a villain through the handlebars of my bicycle! In most western movies, there was always a blacksmith. This person could take pieces of wood, steel…anything, and form it into what was needed to perform a job. They were the parts store and the repair facility all in one. This is very important to remember as the automobile arrives on the scene. There were movies I watched where automobiles were introduced as a rival to the horse. I for one despised these automobiles. Where was the personal connection? I wanted to root for Silver, Trigger, Old Thunder, Tonka, Reno, Arizona, and Dakota...whatever the horse's name was. It was difficult to see this personal touch beaten out by a car! In addition, I could ride a broomstick or bicycle when acting out riding on my favorite horse, how was I to do this for an automobile? We know the automobile eventually won us over. The movie industry realized they could capitalize on this as well with names such as Herby, Ghost Rider, Speed Racer, and so on for cars on the big screen. This is important to remember as car names are more prevalent today than ever and owners want their cars recognized by name. Have you ever noticed a name on a car tag instead of a number? Your customer does not have a 2003 Mustang; they have "THUNDER" or whatever name they have chosen. Many car owners prefer you to call their car by their name. "Mr. Johnson, we have Thunder ready to go."

Back to this blacksmith. I was fortunate to grow up in the 1960s in small town America in Oklahoma where we had three grocery stores, two barber shops, two cafes, two auto parts stores, two clothing/shoe stores, two hardware stores, three full-service gas stations, three automotive repair shops, a movie theater, a jewelry store, a funeral home, a laundry mat and yes, a blacksmith named George. What was amazing is that all of these businesses were independently owned, and they took care of the needs for a town of some 3,000 people. Back to George the blacksmith. I always enjoyed getting to go to George's shop. It smelled funny, not unpleasant just funny. I learned after several visits that this funny smell was coal burning. George used coal to fire his forge and heat the building. I was privileged to watch George on many occasions make and repair plow parts for a man that plowed gardens with a team of beautiful white horses. George made many auto parts for my dad who was a mechanic (technician was not a thought yet nor would I recommend calling an old-time mechanic a technician) when auto parts were not available for a particular job needed. George even took two of our old broken-down bicycles that were doomed for the dump and made a bicycle built for two...and it worked. The point is George could build anything. This was the persona of a blacksmith; they took every job that came in the door knowing it very well could be the only job of the day.

THE OPPORTUNITY

Enter the automobile in the late 1800s. Automakers focused on getting their cars to the public and making them attractive to purchase for the average American. They were not focused on where to find parts when there was a breakdown or where to take these to be repaired. This invention was a direct threat to the blacksmith shop...except for those blacksmiths that realized they must change with the times. These were people that learned to work with their hands, to figure things out and to adapt and conquer whatever new challenge came their way. It was natural that people would turn to this group for auto repair and parts needs on the early automobiles. In turn, many blacksmith shops made the transition to auto repair. As more vehicles hit the road, we began to see full-service gas stations arrive on the scene. These establishments were a work of art! I worked in such a facility while on summer break from high school. You were urgent when you heard the driveway bell ring. You started the gas pump for the $5 of fuel they typically wanted to purchase ($.60 per gallon would get you over 8 gallons) while checking all four tires' pressure, checking "under the hood", which included all fluids and bring the customer a complementary cup of coffee while trying to make it back to the gas pump before it reached $5. We were extremely grateful for the business. Just a funny observation a customer made to me a few years back who owned a full-service station at one time. In his words, "I went to the convenience store this morning, pumped my own gas and paid at the pump, checked my own oil, the TPMS light was on, so I checked my own tires and paid for air, went into the store and paid for a cup of coffee, and I thanked them for being there." This is affirmation that times have certainly changed, and businesses that did not change with the times are no longer around. We must adapt, become adjusted to new conditions daily in our lives.

The pessimist complains about the wind.
The optimist expects it to change.
The leader adjusts the sails.

IMPORTS

As the automobile became popular, the U.S. Federal Government began focusing on things such as safety in 1966, emission pollutants from 1954 – 1970 and energy consumption in 1975 (remember the Oil Embargo). Up until this period, the major automakers were Ford, General Motors, and Chrysler. Now enter Japan. Japan was building smaller cars, which had safety features, met emission pollutant standards and were much better at energy consumption. By 1980, Japan was the largest auto builder in the world. This is how we reacted in the automotive aftermarket. Most repair shops would not work on any import while most auto parts stores and parts manufacturers did not view these Japanese cars as a threat and were sending consumers to the dealerships to get their parts. THAT'LL TEACH 'EM! After all, there were plenty of American made cars to make a living on. Today many brands we called imports in the past are produced in the USA while some U.S. automakers have plants overseas making vehicles.

THE MECHANICAL TIME

When repair on older vehicles became popular, rebuild kits were mostly sold. Master cylinder kits, wheel cylinder kits, tune up kits, rebuilt carburetors, rebuilt engines, etc. Mechanical parts in other words. I became familiar with auto parts and repair in 1974. One of the least desired jobs in both industries was selling a battery as they were all shipped "dry". This meant you had to fill each battery cell with acid and charge the battery, then it was ready to go. What were we filling batteries with? Sulfuric acid, which is a highly corrosive chemical that is potentially explosive in concentrated form. It can cause severe skin burns, can irritate the nose and throat and cause difficulties breathing if inhaled, can burn the eyes and possibly cause blindness, and can burn holes in the stomach if swallowed. Yes, a fourteen-year-old boy was messing with this stuff! In our high school, we had a young man that spilled sulfuric acid on himself accidentally and it caused him to spend weeks in the hospital for burn treatment. The owner of the independent auto parts store I worked for after school had spilled 5 gallons of battery acid on the floor and covered it with oil dry. I swept at night and as I would sweep this area, the concrete floor would continue to break down into a powder and sweep up. When we left that building two years later, the floor was a good 6 inches lower where the acid had been spilled. Auto parts stores and auto repair shops worked with chemicals that were necessary to make parts operate but to also cut through the "gunk" that would build up on parts. Being an auto mechanic was a dangerous and dirty job. Dip your hands into a bucket of carburetor cleaner or spill battery acid on your skin…DANGEROUS. Try to get the smell off from oil, differential fluids, or the smell of exhaust from a lean running carburetor on your cloths and skin…DIRTY. The people that could handle this type of environment made a decent living.

DO IT FOR ME

I decided at the age of 50 that I was going to buy a classic car. Not a fast car just a cool car. I purchased a 1929 Ford Model A Roadster…all original. The previous owner had found and left me a Ford Mechanics Handbook, which was published for the dealerships. There were what we call basics in this book. How to add fluid; adjust brakes, clutch, valves, etc. This was much needed as the average person knew nothing about the automobile repair in 1929. Thus, in the early 1900s enters the automotive mechanic. If you were good at figuring mechanical components out and how they worked, you made a very good mechanic. As independent service stations began working on cars for their customers, this mechanic would figure out how something worked by taking it apart and putting it back together. (No internet to turn to.) As they would figure out how this component worked, they typically would find the defect in the part and repair it. I can remember my dad first starting out in the repair business, trying to draw customers to him. He would take any job to feed the family. I remember the "basket case" jobs. This is where a customer had tried to make a repair himself or herself and realized once the parts were removed that the repair was beyond their skill level. They could not remember how the parts went back together so they would bring them in a container (basket) along with their vehicle usually pulled with a chain by another vehicle. There was a great period of time that most Americans did not have the skill level to perform repairs on their vehicle. This is referred to as the "do it for me" customer.

DO IT YOURSELF

As car owners became more educated to the automobile, the Do It Yourselfer was born. I can remember phone calls my dad received from people asking technical questions so they could repair their vehicle. This was a very disruptive time for shop owners trying to make their living repairing vehicles. It was a no-win situation. If you shared your expertise, you lost a job; if you did not, you lost a friend! As information became more readily available to the public and especially when the World Wide Web arrived, more people began performing repairs at their home. Fortunately, for the modern-day repair facility, vehicles are more complicated, requiring training and specialized tools and equipment to perform repairs. Some motorists may still perform minor repairs and possibly change the oil; however, you now need to be concerned with where you will recycle used fluids to complete a simple oil change at home. We are seeing a trend of Do It for Me business continuing to grow with vehicles becoming more complicated.

THE TECHNICAL TIME

THE 21ST CENTURY

We are living in a very technical time. We must ask ourselves, when did this start? Throughout the mechanical time, ignition systems consisted of a distributor with breaker points and a condenser inside with a distributor cap on top where wires would mount and exit to the spark plugs and an ignition coil externally mounted. Once you grasped the concept, you could work on most all combustion engine ignition systems. Then in the mid 1970s General Motors introduced High Energy Ignition, or HEI as it is commonly called. This consisted of a distributor with a control module replacing the breaker points and condenser and the coil mounted inside the distributor. Automotive mechanics and auto parts stores were faced with a new challenge. Who was going to train the automotive mechanic to now be technical? The natural answer was the parts manufacturers through the auto parts stores since most were reverse engineering original parts to put in their parts line. I know there were some advanced auto parts suppliers that were innovative before this time and already had a team of people making sales calls and training the auto repair facilities. However, many missed a great opportunity when the ignition systems changed, and mechanics needed help understanding this new system. I must say, a good mechanic that understood the combustion engine knew it took three things to fire an engine, fuel, air, and fire (spark). Now one of these components was being delivered in a different way than they knew. (By the way, a combustion engine still requires these three simple ingredients, delivered in different methods with different systems today). Auto parts stores sold many of these mechanics distributors for older models that had the breaker point and condenser set up. Mechanics had figured out a simple way to change the wiring to make an older distributor work on an HEI vehicle. This was not problem solving as much as lack of education in the industry to help everyone understand how this new modern system worked. We should take this learning as Generation 2 ignition as what we knew would be Generation 1. The first vehicles had drum type brakes on all four wheels. Even though disc brakes were first patented in 1902, production did not begin until the 1950s. Today there are still a few cars with drum brakes on the rear. Some changes are instant while others have taken years to evolve. I say that because there have been many changes in the automobile since and many more are sure to come.

THE EARLY DAYS

Auto Parts Stores – Very little upfront or merchandising space. Most stores had concrete blocks with two-by-twelve boards stacked on them to house motor oil. Oil came in a round cardboard can with metal ends in a case of twenty-four. The cans and boxes generally leaked; thus, the boards would absorb the oil. Customers would come to the counter and order the needed part. The parts person would look up the part in a paper catalog, find it on the shelf and charge the customer green sheet price. Stores were not dressed in any particular style, a simple building to conduct business; you got what they had and went on your way. Not much expectation.

Auto Repair Shops – Most early shops had two bays to work in at best. An office desk would be stuck to the side of one of the bays, which is where business was being conducted. Most had a very inappropriate calendar hanging on the wall and the workers (mechanics) were within a few feet of the customers. Language in most shops was "anything goes" and customer service was not a focus; we are here to fix your car, what do you expect? You certainly would not allow women or children to go into these places! As we have progressed into a retail environment, we have learned we must treat people with respect and have a professional attitude toward our business. While this has caused many automotive repair shops to fail, it has created a new persona of the automotive aftermarket business. Many high-quality shops today have a window where customers can see the bays and what is happening to their vehicle. I hope that the following writings will inspire you to take your business to a new level of customer service and professionalism. You will be rewarded once you do!

HOW WE TREAT CUSTOMERS

I am going back to the 1970s for both the auto parts store and the repair facility. Things seemed simpler then. Pricing, for example: There were three price sheets the auto parts store would buy and sell from.

>**BLUE** — Jobber price, which is the price auto parts stores paid for the product.
>
>**SALMON** — Master installer, which is the price the auto parts stores charged the repair facility.
>
>**GREEN** — User, which is the price auto parts stores charged walk-in (DIY) customers.

There was also a published "List" price, which can commonly be called MSRP (Manufacturers Suggested Retail Price) which is the price the repair facility charged their end user.

There was very little deviation to this price strategy. Everyone bought and sold at the same price, almost. Repair facilities would often call the auto parts store to get "green sheet" price and that is what they would charge their customer. After all, they could go directly to the store and get the part for this price. Independent auto parts stores began popping up across America well into the 1980s. As competition and larger auto parts companies began buying up independent stores, this caused a stress on independent automotive parts wholesalers. I can remember that in Tulsa, Oklahoma there were thirteen automotive parts warehouses (wholesalers) in the 1980s. As their customer base began to deteriorate, they looked to the repair shops to fill the void in business. This was a great strategy except this meant that instead of delivering to one auto parts store in each community, they were now delivering to ten to fifteen repair facilities. The dollar sales per delivery were much less while the delivery cost was much higher. The auto repair facility loved the concept as they were now buying parts at jobber price and charging MSRP. The loss of revenue caused the wholesalers to either be acquired or close their business. By the mid 1990s there were no warehouses left in Tulsa.

PEOPLE, WHO NEEDS THEM?

Being a people person is essential for both the auto parts and repair business. If you simply do not like people, this is not for you. I attended a class some years back where the instructor told us that part of selling is acting. What he meant was if you do not care about a person or a situation, you must, at the very least, act as if you do. I disagreed with the instructor then and now. People are smart enough to know when you are not being sincere. People are unique! This is as simple as I can put it. Some people you meet in life, you will have an immediate bond. Others...you will need to work on. If I could go back in time and learn from the people that I disregarded because I did not have that immediate bond, I would be much better for it. That customer that is never wrong or the one that is just difficult to deal with pay with the same form of payment as the customers you have a bond with. In addition, the people you do not see exactly eye to eye with have life lessons you most likely have never considered because of your differences.

I had to have a tough conversation with a friend one time that was difficult. You see, this friend would only allow people that were like them into their life. This was creating a hardship in their life they would not recognize. This person would not even try to consider other people's thoughts if they did not line up with their own. I told this person they were robbing themselves of friendships that could help them in life. Personally, spiritually and in business. I informed this person that if they did not change, they would live a sad and lonely life. I meant this all in love and smiled at this person in the mirror as I finished! You see, the person that can talk to each of us with the most sincere thoughts and facts is ourselves! You must recognize you are not perfect, and neither is anyone else that currently lives on this earth. Uniqueness is what makes this world revolve. Your customers are these unique individuals, and they are looking for you to put forth the effort to get to know and understand them.

SOME OF THE STRANGEST
THINGS HAPPEN

I firmly believe in higher education but also have the utmost respect for life lessons. The stories below, which I have actually experienced, have all taught valuable lessons and hopefully will help you better understand my thoughts on the business side.

Labor claims is a subject the auto parts industry avoids discussing at all costs. This is not my opinion, just the facts from customers and from surveys completed in the automotive aftermarket. Some of the results I have read over the years are as follows: "Technicians are dissatisfied with the current warranty / labor claim system with all suppliers." "Auto parts suppliers view reduction of warranty returns and labor claims as a key factor in improving profits." With these simple remarks, which have been echoed numerous times in different magazine publications, we see there is a point for both sides. Yet, we must realize this is something real and it has effects on both sides of the business. With this said, we must be talking about warranty

/ labor claim from the auto parts stores to the automotive shops. This is a real issue and not going away, so I will share a simple story on why it is important to discuss. I was an outside salesperson at the time this incident occurred and visited this particular customer weekly. As I arrived at the auto parts store, I was informed this customer had a response from a fuel pump manufacturer on four fuel pumps that were returned as warranty / labor claim for the same vehicle. In the response there was a Technical Service Bulletin stating the baffle in the fuel tank could come loose and move to where it would cover the fuel pump and starve it for fuel, thus overheating the pump causing the pump to fail. The technical service bulletin was also included in every fuel pump box for this part number, but who reads what is in the box, right? It was my job to relay this information to the customer. As I entered the customer's business, they were waiting for me! You can guess what was in the bay, the same vehicle back for fuel pump number five. The owner informed me, "We have a problem!" I told the customer I knew about the issue and had a document to read from the manufacturer. The customer raised their eyebrows toward me, and I told them I was going to work with them regardless of what the document said. As I was reading the document, the technician that had replaced all the fuel pumps became very agitated at the shop owner to a point I thought it was going to get physical. Stating, "I told you something was loose in the tank the first time we did this." We worked out a deal where I helped the customer secure a fuel tank at a discount and the fuel pump manufacturer gave credit on the fuel pumps. What would happen if this labor claim had not been discussed with the customer? My company would be out of pocket on parts and labor money with the issue still not resolved for the vehicle owner.

Good notes matter. I had an issue to deal with from an outside salesperson stating a customer had purchased a piece of equipment then the customer's wife passed away and he was going to close his business. The question was, could we help them with the equipment they no longer have a need for. The answer is, "Of course, we will do everything we can to help this customer." I took charge of the situation and called the customer to discuss options, and to my surprise, his dead wife answered the phone. The real story is the wife had some medical issues that needed special treatment, which was a several hour drive away, so they were selling the business to move closer to where her treatments were to be performed. I am certainly glad the customer himself did not answer the phone and I gave my condolences for the passing of his wife! Good notes deliver good information, or maybe in this case someone was trying to be as tragic and sympathetic as possible to ensure I would "take care" of them. In the end, we sold the equipment for the customer, and they came out very well. In addition, they opened a shop at their new location, and we got their business because they knew we would be there through the good and the bad.

Pricing is something we are challenged with no matter if it is the parts or the repair side of the business. On the parts side one of my greatest thrills was working for a growing company that was building stores into areas where the customers were not familiar with the company name. I enjoyed the calls to repair shops to introduce our company and solicit business. On returning calls, I was told at different times we were "too high" on our prices. When investigating further from the customer input and talking to the store personnel, there was never a communication from the customer to check our prices to begin with. Why would a customer tell me this when they had not even checked our prices? The answer is simple, to make me go away! There was something the customer did not like about my company or me, and since there was not a relationship at this point it had to be hearsay. This is when you learn to go slow with the customer, keep calling on them but not as often. Build a relationship slowly and teach the customer about yourself and the company.

I am also reminded of times when "perception" gets in the way of reality on pricing. I was visiting a shop where the store person I was working with told me the customer was price conscious on everything, but we were selling them some items. As we walked in, the customer asked the store person, "Is this the guy that is going to fix my pricing?" The store person said yes and walked off to another part of the shop leaving me to discuss pricing with a person I was meeting for the first time. I asked the customer what issues he was having with pricing. He was leaning on a car and said, "I need a hub bearing for this car and I can get it for $49.99 from one of your competitors." I knew the competitor he was talking of. They stocked a short line, ten part numbers of a very cheaply made hub bearing to "get their foot in the door" with repair facilities. I asked why the customer did not already get the bearing from our competitor to which he replied, "They are out of it, and it will take two weeks to get it." I told the customer we did not have a $49.99 hub bearing. I also said that I would be happy to have a bearing delivered and I would show the features and benefits of our bearing and the obvious differences. The customer told me that would be fine if I sold the bearing to him for $49.99. Our price was

$74.99 for the bearing, which the customer already knew. Again, I said I could show *why* my bearing costs more, which are the features and benefits of the bearing. This game went on for around ten minutes when the customer said, "You are not hearing me, I need a $49.99 bearing." To which I replied, "You did not say that, you were trying to get me to discount my quality bearing to the price of the cheap bearing. I can get you a $49.99 bearing and it would take about two weeks to get it." I knew I was pushing the limits at this point but also, I was having fun with the customer, and I could tell he was having fun with me. What the customer said next really sets the tone for defending your product. The customer said, "Send me your bearing for $74.99. I have not quoted my customer a price at this point, so price is not a big deal." What is the reason the customer wanted to challenge price? Very simple, nobody from my company had defended our product line up and price. We had simply been losing business due to price with the perception that quality was the same.

On the shop side, we reached a point in our repair business where oil changes created a large part of our revenue. We had a major retailer in our area who also performed oil changes. This company sent representatives to our shop to get pricing on every service we offered. At the time, which was in the early 1990s, our oil change was $20 for up to 5 quarts of oil and a new filter on a gasoline engine including tax. Our retail competitor began advertising their oil change for $13.88 plus tax for "the same service". We had a few customers that would ask what the difference was in our $20 oil change and their $15 oil change (after tax). The correct answer is not $5 in this case, although I often had the urge to say that. When faced with a comparison, human nature is to talk about us versus them. This is not a good way to serve your customers. I had a "canned" response I would give customers. "Here is what we do, we vacuum your interior, check *all* applicable fluids (transmission, anti-freeze, differential, etc.), check the air filter, fill the wiper fluid reservoir, ensure proper air pressure in all four tires, place a custom disposable trash bag in the vehicle, spray deodorizer in the interior, change the oil filter with a quality name brand, drain and fill the crankcase with the appropriate amount of motor oil of your choice, grease any applicable chassis zerts and deliver your vehicle within fifteen minutes while you wait." I would always attempt to give this answer in one breath! When I was asked what the competition did, my answer was always, "I don't know what services they provide, you would need to ask them." Although, I knew the competition changed the crankcase oil with a bulk oil, no choices, and replaced the oil filter while the customer shopped for several hours in their retail store. That was their business model and it worked for them. In all the time of dealing with this, which was a couple of years, we lost one customer to the competition. After two years of competing with this retailer, we learned their service center was now the "Garden Center". They stopped performing oil changes completely.

How to NOT offend a customer! Who would know the most about a vehicle, the people that build the vehicle or the experienced technician? This brings me to a vehicle I had purchased that had a factory warranty. Part of the stipulation of the warranty was to have all service intervals performed at the appropriate times. It came time for my vehicle to have the transmission serviced so I took it to a very good customer who owned a respectable repair business. I told the shop owner what service I needed and was shocked at his response. "I won't do it! That is crazy to change the fluid at only 30,000 miles. You are wasting your money!" I replied that I wanted the service performed to keep my factory warranty active. This person would not budge; he refused to perform the service. I took the vehicle across the street to his competitor to have the service performed. The service intervals recommended by the factory is what I went by and was being ridiculed for asking.

PROBLEM SOLVING

Any time you are in a service-related business, you must look at it as taking a problem from your customer and returning a product to the customer that is no longer a problem. Pretty simple! When my car is breaking down, I am in panic mode. How am I going to get the kids to school, get myself to work, get to my hair appointment, get groceries then pick the kids up from school? What we cannot do is to tell the customer, "Don't make your problems my problems!" Think of going to a restaurant and the food you ordered is not cooked as you had instructed. You do not go to the kitchen and talk to the cook; you complain to the wait staff. You make your problem their problem, even though they did not make the mistake. Your expectation is that the person serving you is the person responsible for everything, whether good or bad that happens during your visit. This is the same expectation your customer has of you! Below is a neat story of turning problems around.

A daughter constantly complained to her father that her life was miserable and that she did not know how she was going to make it. She was tired of fighting and struggling all the time. It seemed just as one problem was solved, another one soon followed.

Her father, a chef, took her to the kitchen. He filled three pots with water and placed each on a high fire. Once the three pots began to boil, he placed potatoes in one pot, eggs in the second pot, and ground coffee beans in the third pot.

He then let them sit and boil, without saying a word to his daughter. The daughter moaned and impatiently waited, wondering what he was doing.

After twenty minutes he turned off the burners. He took the potatoes out of the pot and placed them in a bowl. He pulled the boiled eggs out and placed them in a bowl.

He then ladled the coffee out and placed it in a cup. Turning to his daughter, he asked, "What do you see?"

"Potatoes, eggs, and coffee," she hastily replied.

"Look closer," he said, "and touch the potatoes." She did and noted that they were soft. He then asked her to take an egg and break it. After pulling off the shell, she observed the hard-boiled egg. Finally, he asked her to sip the coffee. Its rich aroma brought a smile to her face.

"What does this mean?" she asked.

He then explained that the potatoes, the eggs, and coffee beans had each faced the same adversity—the boiling water.

However, each one reacted differently.

The potato went in strong, hard, and unrelenting, but in boiling water, it became soft and weak.

The egg was fragile, with the thin outer shell protecting its liquid interior until it was placed in the boiling water. Then the inside of the egg became hard.

However, the ground coffee beans were unique. After they were exposed to the boiling water, they changed the water and created something new.

"Which are you," he asked his daughter. "When adversity knocks on your door, how do you respond? Are you a potato, an egg, or a coffee bean? "

Moral: In life, things happen around us, things happen to us, but the only thing that truly matters is what happens within us.

Which one are you?

HONESTY

It is amazing the number of repair shops that "add on" items customers do not need. There is such a vast amount of legitimate add on sales that will actually help the customer that it astonishes me how many times the customer gets additional charges they do not need. If you have ever heard "what goes around, comes around", please read the stories below.

There was a farmer who regularly sold butter to a baker. One day, the baker decided to weigh the butter to see if he was getting the exact amount that he asked for. He found out that he was not, so he took the farmer to court.

The judge asked the farmer if he uses any measure to weigh the butter. The farmer replied, "Your Honor, I'm primitive. I don't have a proper measure, but I do have a scale."

The judge replied, "Then how do you weigh the butter?"

The farmer replied, "Your Honor, long before the baker started buying butter from me, I have been buying a pound loaf of bread from him. Every day, when the baker brings the bread,

I put it on the scale and give him the same weight in butter. If anyone is to be blamed, it's the baker."

Moral of the story: In life, you get what you give. Do not try to cheat others.

One night four college kids stayed out late, partying and having a good time. They paid no mind to the test they had scheduled for the next day and did not study. In the morning, they hatched a plan to get out of taking their test. They covered themselves with grease and dirt and went to the Dean's office. Once there, they said they had been to a wedding the previous night and on the way back they got a flat tire and had to push the car back to campus.

The Dean listened to their tale of woe and thought. He offered them a retest three days later. They thanked him and accepted his offer.

When the test day arrived, they went to the Dean. The Dean put them all in separate rooms for the test. They were fine with this since they had all studied hard. Then they saw the test. It had two questions.

YOUR NAME _____ (1 Points)

WHICH TIRE BURST? _____ (99 Points)

OPTIONS — (a) Front Left

(b) Front Right

(c) Back Left

(d) Back Right

BUILDING AN AUTOMOTIVE REPAIR BUSINESS

Before you make any decision about opening a business, you must first examine yourself and the commitment you are going to need for such an endeavor. I am reminded of a true story I will share.

How do you define true commitment? Let me tell you how Hernan Cortes defined it. In 1519, under the sponsorship of Cuba's Governor Velasquez, Cortes sailed from Cuba to the Mexican mainland with the goal of gaining riches for Spain and fame for himself. Only thirty-four years old, the young Spanish captain had prepared his whole life for such a chance.

However, the soldiers under his command were not as dedicated as he. After he landed, there was talk that the men might mutiny and return to Cuba with his ships. What was his solution? He burned the ships. How dedicated are you and your team? Are you totally committed, or do you have an "out", just in case things do not work out? Remember, there is no such thing as a halfhearted champion.

WARNING

Before you proceed with reading the following, you must determine if you are going to be a legitimate competitive business. I know this sounds like a dumb topic, so let me explain. When I was a small child, my grandfather owned and operated a coin laundry mat. We lived just a block away from the downtown area, which was where most of the businesses were at that time, so I frequented the laundry. In fact, at a very young age my first job was sweeping the sidewalk in front of the laundry after school. I think I earned something like fifty cents per day. That was enough to hit the Coke and candy machine every day, with change left over. As I grew into a young teen, I can remember an event where my dad received a phone call from my grandfather asking my dad if he could come watch the laundry mat as my grandfather met with a man that was interested in purchasing the business. The meeting occurred off site and when my grandfather came back in, he asked my dad if he could stay a little longer, he needed to run home because the man interested wanted to see his "books" on the business. Certain things burn into your mind over a lifetime that you remember. These are the simplest and at the time, meaningless things. I remember my dad asking, "You leave the books at home?" To which my grandfather replied, "No, I need to go home and make them!" There are a vast number of businesses that do not want "Uncle Sam" knowing the volume they actually do in business to avoid paying as much income tax. I can also remember a lot of these people, whether they were tree trimmers, mechanics, retail business owners, etc. complaining after they retired about the ridiculously low amount they were receiving in social security benefits.

So, what does that have to do with an automotive repair business? I have had the fortune of visiting literally thousands of repair shops over my years. When new technology is introduced to the automobile, there is typically equipment and training required to the aftermarket to repair these vehicles. I have had too many shop owners tell me they are not going to upgrade their equipment because... One "because" has always been, "I am not going to do this much longer, so I am not updating." What happens when this shop owner decides to do something different or retire? They want to sell their "business". The problem is they have a building (maybe) and outdated equipment. They do not really have what they thought was a business, just old material possessions that are worth a fraction of what they paid. Let us see what an interested party would be looking for in purchasing a business. Does the potential seller have quality employees that would stay with the new owner? Unfortunately, when a shop gets to this point, the owner is the only person left in the business. "Show me your books!" I want to see your customer base, marketing strategy, equipment, the year make and model of vehicles the equipment can diagnose and yes, if the business is profitable. What owners in this category must understand is, "You have nothing to sell!" Therefore, they end up having a garage sale and the potential buyer opens their own repair facility and starts from scratch, which is easier than sifting through the business they purchased only to find out it was not a business after all. If you are starting a brand-new repair facility, which a person can make a very good income doing, make sure it is a business and you have all the equipment and resources to present yourself as a true business owner. If you fit into the category of already owning a repair facility but have not kept current on technology, it is gut check time. You need either to invest in your business or do something else to earn a living because your "business" is dying a slow death. I know there are a number of very efficiently operated repair shops that are saying AMEN to this. These inefficient shops are causing the good shops to spend a lot of time explaining to customers the difference in what they do versus the inefficient shop down the street.

How you carry yourself is how you are perceived. The same is true for your business! A true story about an everyday cab driver that changed the course of his life.

No one can make you serve customers well...that is because great service is a choice. Here is a wonderful story about a cab driver that proved this point.

A man was waiting in line for a ride at the airport. When a cab pulled up, the first thing the man noticed was the taxi polished to a bright shine. Smartly dressed in white shirt, black tie, and freshly pressed black slacks, the cab driver jumped out and rounded the car to open the back passenger door for the man...

He handed the man a laminated card and said, "I'm Will, your driver. While I'm loading your bags in the trunk, I'd like you to read my mission statement."

Taken aback, the man read the card... It said, "Will's Mission Statement: To get my customers to their destination in the quickest, safest, and cheapest way possible in a friendly environment..."

This blew the man away. Especially when he noticed the inside of the cab matched the outside. Spotlessly clean! As he slid behind the wheel, Will said, "Would you like a cup of coffee? I have a thermos of regular and one of decaf." The man said jokingly, "No, I'd prefer a soft drink." Will smiled and said, "No problem, I have a cooler in front with regular and Diet Coke, water, and orange juice..." Almost stuttering, the man said, "I'll take a Diet Coke." Handing him his drink, Will said, "If you'd like something to read, I have *The Wall Street Journal*, *Time*, *Sports Illustrated* and *USA Today*." As they were pulling away, Will handed the man another laminated card. "These are the stations I get and the music they play, if you'd like to listen to the radio." In addition, as if that were not enough, Will said that he had the air conditioning on and asked if the temperature was comfortable for him. Then he advised the man of the best route to his destination for that time of day. He also let him know that he would be happy to chat and tell him about some of the sights or, if the man preferred, to leave him with his own thoughts. "Tell me, Will," the amazed man asked the driver, "have you always served customers like this?"

Will smiled into the rear-view mirror. "No, not always... In fact, it has only been in the last two years. My first five years driving, I spent most of my time complaining like all the rest of the cabbies do. Then I heard a personal growth guru on the radio one day. He had just written a book. He said that if you get up in the morning expecting to have a bad day you will rarely disappoint yourself. He said, 'Stop complaining! Differentiate yourself from your competition. Do not be a duck. Be an eagle. Ducks quack and complain. Eagles soar above the crowd....'

"That hit me right between the eyes," said Will. "He was really talking about me. I was always quacking and complaining, so I decided to change my attitude and become an eagle. I looked around at the other cabs and their drivers. The cabs were dirty, the drivers were unfriendly, and the customers were unhappy. Therefore, I decided to make some changes. I put in a few at a time. When my customers responded well, I did more."

"I take it that has paid off for you," the man asked. "It sure has," Will replied. "My first year as an eagle, I doubled my income from the previous year. This year I will probably quadruple it.

"You were lucky to get me today. I do not sit at cabstands anymore. My customers call me for appointments on my cell phone or leave a message on my answering machine. If I can't pick them up myself, I get a reliable cabbie friend to do it and I take a piece of the action." Will was phenomenal. He was running a limo service out of a Yellow Cab.

A man reaps what he sows. Let us not become weary in doing good, for at the proper time we will reap a harvest if we do not give up... let us do good to all people. "Life isn't about waiting for the storm to pass. It's about learning to dance in the rain."

LOCATION

While there are some things that are a given (equipment, tools, office space, etc.), there are also some requirements to survive in this business that are often overlooked. In building any new business, location drives the type of customer you are attempting to attract. Sometimes it can drive the customer to you while there are times your location will drive the customer away. Over the years, I have seen many repair facilities built away from where the major traffic travels. I am not saying a business in this type of area cannot survive, but you do need to determine what type of customer you are trying to attract. If you are building your business in the area of a factory or office complex, you can attract the employees of the businesses around you.

To be convenient, you may need to offer free pick up and drop off or a shuttle service. Making it convenient for your customer to have their vehicle maintained or repaired while they are at work will make your customer feel at ease. This also means most jobs will need to be completed before the customer is off work, so they are not inconvenienced for their commute home.

Hours of operation depend on the hours of operation of the places from where you are drawing your business. I have seen many great repair facilities do a fantastic business in areas such as this. The downside is your business depends on the success of other businesses around you. If there is a layoff, shut down, the business closes for weeks or months every year, your business will be directly affected. Having a captured audience has advantages and disadvantages. You can be successful but there should be a lot of planning around building your business in this manner.

Building a business in a heavy retail area will offer you the largest customer base. Finding demographics of the area should always be your first step. Your real estate agent can assist you with this. You are going to want to know the average income, average age of automobiles, type of automobiles, etc. that are around you. Analytics is a great thing; it can give you a road map of what to expect, how to market and who to market to in the area you are looking at. One thing that has always puzzled me is when a technician leaves a shop to start his or her own business. They seem to generally have the knowhow, tools, etc. to repair vehicles. However, they do not know where their customer base is coming from or a business plan. When a technician leaves a successful business to start their own, the customers are not necessarily going to follow them. Change causes discomfort for customers and discomfort is avoided. You must draw your customer base to you; simply opening the door will not cause interest in you or your business.

If you are in the auto parts business, please take note of the "nuggets" of information listed inside the following. This can greatly help you understand your customer and their expectations.

HOURS OF OPERATION

This subject is one of the most painful for our industry. We would all love to have an 8-5 job Monday - Friday. However, retail demands you be available when the customer has free time to have service work completed. Working on both sides of the business (auto parts and auto repair), the repair side should have learned from the parts side from some changes that were required for the auto parts store to remain in business. Hours of operation is one of the hot points.

NUGGET: When you are choosing an auto parts provider, their hours of operation should also be considered. Do they have a dedicated commercial counter with their best parts person working it? What hours does this person work? What happens when you need a part beyond this person's operating hours?

Back to your hours, demographics and traffic count can assist you with this. What hours are the heaviest traffic hours? Is the major traffic during weekdays between 7:00 A.M. and 8:00 A.M. in the morning and 5:00 P.M. and 6:00 P.M. in the evening?

Then you are in a working class of customer's area and probably need to open extended hours during the week and on Saturday's to be convenient for the customer's needs. If there are fleet customers in the area, (plumbing companies, construction companies, etc.) you have a great opportunity to fill your bays on the weekdays. A good mix of retail and fleet can always keep your shop full. Who will you be competing with in this market? National chains have great success in retail environments, but you can compete and win against them. Consideration of the above will help your business meet the expectations of the market.

STAFFING

Once you have determined the market demographics, you can establish what type of staffing is required. Your staff should coincide with the type of services you are providing. For example, if you will be performing drivability, you will need a Master Technician. However, if your area were one that you will be performing maintenance (fluid flushes, filters, oil changes, etc.) a less experienced technician would be all that is required. Once you have the demographics of the area, you can determine the types of services required for the area. Having a Service Advisor that is well versed in the automotive system with access to a great shop management system (Mitchell 1, ALL DATA, etc.) will make the bay flow smoothly. However, be careful how you compensate this position.

> **NUGGET:** For example, if the Service Advisor is paid a commission on parts sales, this can cause the flow into the bays to slow down. To explain, if the service advisor is paid a commission on the difference in selling price and cost

of parts, they are going to shop around every time for the best price. Therefore, while they are trying to put more money in their pocket, they are leaving technicians standing around waiting on parts. This causes inefficiencies in the workflow, which is the number one reason technicians leave. It is frustrating standing around waiting when there is work to do and vehicles backed up.

As you are looking at staffing your business, you must consider the competition in the market. Things such as employee benefits, caliber of technicians and longevity on the job will tell you whether the shop that employs these people are successful. Do you have an insurance program, paid time off, bonus program, etc.? This is what it takes to compete for the best.

> **NUGGET:** When choosing a parts provider, choose one than can help you with this. Several do have programs available.

Will technicians have training available to remain current with new technology?

> **NUGGET:** Your parts provider should have a program available…choose your parts provider carefully! Ensuring every technician understands training is a requirement and paid for by the company (you) is critical. It is simple to have a "Lunch & Learn" monthly in house. Look for short virtual classes or ask your parts provider for a representative that can give a constructive 30-minute discussion on a particu-

lar subject.

For lack of training,

They lacked knowledge.

For lack of knowledge,

They lacked confidence.

For lack of confidence,

They lacked victory.

Julius Caesar

You will want to establish written policies for your company. It does not matter the number of employees you have, there must be clarity in everything you do.

Mission statement: whether you are a small or large company, you should share your vision with your employees and your customers.

Goal setting: When people have goals, they literally have a measuring stick. Every position should have goals to reach along with compensation for reaching the goals and penalties for not reaching the goals. This will help greatly when conducting performance evaluations. A road map of expectations and how the employee performed is much better than basing expectations on feelings.

MARKETING

To simply describe marketing, it is how you are going to attract new customers and retain current customers. We live in an electronic age. The majority of customers have proven they want contact via e-mail or social media. A good shop management system should have an option for social media marketing. You want a system that is competitive, one that will allow scheduling, marketing campaigns, reviews, vehicle service history, service reminders, etc.

> **NUGGET:** Find a supplier that offers a shop management system and will participate in allowing you to earn back all or a portion of your shop management system fees through parts purchases, and one that participates in marketing campaigns that will drive customers to your business.

Do not allow a system to take the place of human interaction… If you have ever had a service performed and receive a phone call the following day from the shop asking if your expectations were met, you feel this establishment really cares about you! Between demographics and a customer retention program (shop management system), you have a source of finding new customers and drawing them into your facility. There seems to be an argument whether flyers mailed are still effective. Do not dismiss any opportunity until you know what works in your area. Without having a person taking ownership and monitoring all communication, it is useless to invest. Staying active with what happened yesterday, today, and tomorrow is essential. You could get a reply on a review stating the customer's vehicle had grease on the floor mat when they picked it up and they will never return. The best system in the world cannot replace a human contacting this customer offering to correct the situation. You only get one shot in most cases.

LOOK IN UNUSUAL PLACES FOR IDEAS

Good leaders are attentive to ideas; they are always searching for them. In addition, they cultivate that attentiveness and practice it as a regular discipline. As they read the newspaper, watch a movie, listen to their colleagues, or enjoy a leisure activity, they are always on the lookout for ideas or practices they can use to improve their work and their leadership. If you desire to find good ideas, you must search for them. Rarely does a good idea come looking for you.

CUSTOMER SERVICE

As the automotive aftermarket has traveled through the ages, it has opened up to more women as the decision makers on their automobiles. This is from purchasing a vehicle to servicing it. There is some debate on what the actual percentage of female vs male drivers there are, so to keep it simple I will use a very conservative number of 50%.

Now, when I talk to shop owners and tell them a number such as this, I get a reply of "50% of my business is not female." Therefore, I wait for it... then they figure it out. This means they are missing 50% of their market entitlement!

A professional appearance and atmosphere are required for both male and female customers. You will want an attractive women's rest room, as that is what is required. Remember to ALWAYS respect the woman as the decision maker for their vehicle. With all customers you must always FIX IT RIGHT THE FIRST TIME, DELIVER WHEN PROMISED, HAVE A CLEAN ENVIRONMENT FOR CUSTOMERS, RESPECT THE CUSTOMER, and BE COMPETITIVELY

PRICED. Notice I did not say be the cheapest, you are paid to perform a highly technical service on the second most expensive asset most families own. Your customers will teach you how they expect to be treated.

21st CENTURY LOBBY / WAITING ROOM

If customers will be waiting on their vehicle in your facility, they have certain expectations for the area where they will be waiting. You can build a simple Word document survey form to ask customers to complete. Their doctors and dentists already have them trained to do this, so a form is all you need. Make it simple, below is an example.

I PREFER TO DRINK _____

I PREFER TO READ _____

I PREFER TO WATCH _____ ON THE TELEVISION

I PREFER WIFI AVAILABILITY Y/N

I TAKE MY CHILDREN WITH ME WHEREVER I GO Y/N

(This will tell you if you need children's activities to keep them busy)

I WANT A WARRANTY Y/N

I ONLY WANT THE REPAIR I CAME FOR COMPLETED Y/N

I DON'T WANT TO HAVE ADDITIONAL PROBLEMS LATER Y/N

DOES YOUR VEHICLE HAVE A NAME? Y/N

IF YES, WHAT IS THE NAME?

_____

SELLING

The modern automobile is more technical than it has ever been with most DIY customers not having the knowledge to perform maintenance let alone repairs. We discussed training earlier, showing your qualifications, and selling your qualifications. You want to be known as the shop that RE-QUIRES training. You keep your team up to date with the latest technology. Showing your qualifications is a huge VALUE for the customer. Value has nothing to do with price...unless you do not show the value. You do not want a customer calling you saying you charged them too much, and now you begin telling them about the differences in your business and what you do to ensure the correct procedures are followed to repair their vehicle. WHY? Because 1 in 10 will call back while 9 will not call or come back!

Unfortunately, we are in the pain business. When a vehicle breaks down, a repair is not what the customer intended to spend their money on. Some things can make the customer feel better about the repair. Perception is reality. It does not matter

that you have a well-trained staff and great customer service…
if the customer does not feel this then their perception is that
you do not!

NEVER DIAGNOSE A VEHICLE AT THE COUNTER OR OVER THE PHONE

It is impossible to diagnose the modern automobile without
having the vehicle in your presence. Explain diagnostics to the
customer. Many will ask, "Do you have one of those machines
that will tell you what is wrong with my car?" That is the perception of a lot of people.

NEVER EXCEED YOUR ESTIMATE

When a customer pays less than estimated, they feel you have
their best interest in mind. When a customer pays more than
estimated, it causes distrust.

SHOW YOUR QUALIFICATIONS

Showing a certificate of the technician that will be repairing the
vehicle and explaining they recently attended a class on the
exact problem the customer is explaining sets the customer at
ease. You know what you are doing!

SHOW YOUR VALUE

Ensure the customer knows everything you do to vehicles, you
keep them safe and secure while in your possession and any ex-
tras (vacuum, wash windows, etc.) you include.

SHOW YOUR WARRANTY

NUGGET: It is simple to offer a nationwide warranty today. Any major auto parts supplier can assist you with this. You must explain, this is YOUR warranty (the repair facility) and even if they are traveling and you cannot get to them, you have a network of quality repair facilities nationwide you have partnered with to take care of warranties.

DO NOT TALK TECHNICAL TO THE CUSTOMER

Talk such as EGR, ECM, TPS, IAC...are confusing. Instead, have a printout ready from your shop management system to show the customer what repair you performed. With pictures!

ALWAYS DELIVER WHEN PROMISED

When the customer calls or shows up, know when you promised the car (shop management system) and that, "of course, your vehicle is ready".

NUGGET: Pick a parts supplier that has a representative that comes to your business on a regular basis. Someone that is interested in your business succeeding, someone that does not talk about other repair facilities in your area. SOMEONE YOU TRUST! With that said, trust is built on experience, so it will require a building process. I say this so you can realize you need a parts provider that retains people and you do not have a "flavor of the month" salesperson or someone new to build trust with every week, month or year. You want a trusting relationship to where this representative can tell you that your building front is ugly and driving business away for the lack of repair. I have experienced so many "sales" people over the years that I began putting them in "buckets" as I met them. This is included later as I discuss auto parts salespeople.

PHONE ETIQUETTE

Ensure any person that could potentially answer the phone is trained with the proper way you expect it to be answered.

FRIENDLY GREETING

You must determine the standard greeting you expect. "Thank you for calling Ron's Auto, how can I help you?"

LISTEN AND LEARN

Give the caller 100% of your attention while listening intently.

FEATURES AND BENEFITS

Name your typical features and benefits—shuttle service, waiting room, courtesy car, warranty, etc.

ASK FOR THE SALE

"When would you like to bring your vehicle in?"

FOLLOW UP

A simple call back on the progress you have made will cause a customer to feel at ease. If not, the customer will be paranoid waiting on you: "I wonder what is wrong with my car? How much is this going to cost? How long will I be without my car?"

INSPECTIONS

Dealerships have been the winners on these

Every customer wants to feel confident their vehicle will be safe and reliable once they have it repaired. Develop an inspection form and process to cover with the customer. Customers would rather hear: "We performed an inspection, and your vehicle needs a cabin air filter…" They do not want to get down the road and learn from someone else that they need something when "you should have caught that".

Identify factory maintenance intervals (shop management system) and have that as part of your inspection. Your customer should not need to go to the dealership to learn there is a TSB (technical service bulletin) for their vehicle. A good shop management system will have this feature. The same with service intervals.

WHY MAINTENANCE SERVICE

- Not a pain sale

- Do not need a highly experienced technician to perform
- High profit margin
- Saves the vehicle owner money
- Promotes vehicle longevity
- Keeps factory warranty current
- Better vehicle performance
- Higher vehicle resale value
- Reduces stress—not a crisis repair
- Promotes long term customer loyalty
- Improves shop scheduling

SERVICE WRITER / ADVISOR

This is a critical position in your business! Customers need a "face" of the business. This is where a service writer or advisor fits. You want a dynamic and positive personality talking to your customers. This person must be skilled at multitasking, take great notes and have excellent follow up skills. Remember a large population of DIFM business are women, you must consider this when choosing this position. This position also dictates the efficiency in the bays.

A few years back, I began talking to technicians that were leaving a shop or had recently moved from one shop to another. One simple question, why did you or are you making a move? The answer was astounding... Inefficiency in getting jobs from the front counter to the bay! In other words, there was plenty of work to be completed. The technicians were standing around waiting on the service advisor to assign jobs. Assigning each job to the most experienced technician for that particular job will increase bay productivity. If they are the person ordering parts, are they getting the parts to the technicians in a timely manner?

Customer callbacks and approvals must happen efficiently so bay productivity remains moving. Upselling maintenance service and getting the vehicle from the technician performing repairs to the technician performing maintenance in a timely manner is critical. Be sure you understand the topic under staffing about carefully choosing how you pay this position.

Maintenance sales are a great way to incentivize. We must get over the idea that we know more than the vehicle manufacturer, for example if a 2020 Chevrolet Colorado recommends cleaning the fuel injectors at 25,000 miles, we do not want to tell the customer, "I feel that is too soon." This a very simple conversation, "Your vehicle manufacturer recommends the fuel injectors are cleaned at 25,000 miles." Your customer can easily look on their vehicle service manual and see this is a fact! Where are you going to get this information? Directly from your shop management system... If you have not figured out by now, this is a major tool for running your business!

So, in short, your service advisor WILL make or break your business...CHOOSE WISELY! This person must be highly organized and an excellent time manager.

Imagine you had a bank account that deposited $86,400 each morning. The account carries over no balance from day to day, allows you to keep no cash balance, and every evening cancels whatever part of the amount you had failed to use during the day. What would you do? Draw out every dollar each day!

We all have such a bank. Its name is Time. Every morning, it credits you with 86,400 seconds. Every night it writes off, as lost, whatever time you have failed to use wisely. It carries over no balance from day to day. It allows no overdraft so you cannot borrow against yourself or use more time than you have. Each day, the account starts fresh. Each night, it destroys all unused time. If you fail to use the day's deposits, it is your loss, and you cannot appeal to get it back.

There is never any borrowing time. You cannot take a loan out on your time or against someone else's. The time you have is the time you have and that is that. Time management is yours to decide how you spend the time, just as with money you decide how you spend the money. It is never a case of us not having enough time to do things, but the case of whether we want to do them and where they fall in our priorities.

A common obstacle to success is the desire to cut corners and take the short road to success. Shortcuts never pay off in the long run. As Napoleon said, victory belongs to the most persevering. Most people tend to underestimate the time it takes to achieve something of value, but to be successful you must be willing to pay your dues.

James Watt spent twenty years laboring to perfect his steam engine.

William Harvey labored night and day for eight years to prove how blood circulated in the human body. It took another twenty-five years for the medical profession to acknowledge he was right.

Cutting corners is a sign of impatience and poor self-discipline. If you are willing to follow through, you can achieve a breakthrough. If you continually give in to your moods or impulses, then you need to change your approach to doing things. The best method is to set standards for yourself that require accountability. Suffering a consequence for not following through helps you stay on track. Once you have your new standards in place, work according to them, not your moods. That will get you going in the right direction. Do what does not come naturally!

CHOOSING A PARTS SUPPLIER

This is a critical decision in your business. This is literally a decision of marrying two companies together for the good of both, so choose your bride wisely! You should look at your parts supplier as a partner in your business. You are not looking for someone that drops by with "specials" periodically. You should look for someone that has a regiment and is in your shop weekly, the same day and around the same time. I highly recommend creating an interview process for a supplier and the salesperson. The best shops have a very intimate business relationship with their supplier, knowing when the representative is in their business, and will be there with ideas and programs that will help drive or retain shop business. I would also ensure the supplier knows to bring their entire program to the interview. You do not want them running back and forth to gather information for you. This will show you how engaged with their company programs this person is. You are going to want to know the following:

- Tell me about your product line up. You want features, benefits, quality, availability and warranty.
- Tell me about your programs. This could take a while to cover but it is very important, as there will be programs that benefit you, that your parts supplier is paying for.
  - Service Center Program
    - Nationwide Warranty
    - Local Labor Claim Warranty
    - Personalized Branding for Your Business (external websites, signage, specials, etc.)
    - Outside Partnerships with Providers to Market Your Business, (this could allow you additional discounts with training, uniforms, insurance, and computer hardware, regional and national agencies…)
    - Consumer Financing
    - Tire Warranty (if you sell tires)
    - Commercial Vehicle Warranty
  - Technician & Service Writer Training
  - Electronic Ordering & Incentives (Is the parts provider connected with a shop management provider?)
- Payment terms
  - Method of payment on account allowed
  - Early payment discounts
  - Rebates
- Equipment Program
  - Can you depend on this supplier for all your business needs?
  - Do they have an equipment earn back program?
- Pricing

- You are not looking for the "cheapest", you are looking for the best value which includes every program offered and a fair price on parts.
- Store Team & Service Expectations
  - What is a realistic delivery time?
  - How often are returns picked up?
  - Who will be your go-to person at the store and what is their experience?
  - What hours of operation can you expect a go-to person to be available?
  - You want to hear comments about how they are dedicated to keeping your bays turning, not about how great they are. The focus must be on YOUR customer service.
  - You should have your realistic expectations ready.

When in the repair business, I called our supplier for a serpentine belt with a customer waiting. I was told their driver was getting ready to take a delivery and would get the belt added with me being the first stop. I should have the belt within ten minutes. I removed the old belt as my customer was in a hurry to get out of town and I needed to accommodate. I looked out our bay door and saw the supplier's truck coming, getting closer and drove on by. I ordered the belt from my supplier's competitor whom we did no business with, and it arrived in fifteen minutes. I had now held my customer up for thirty minutes when I told them fifteen minutes based on the information I was given. I charged the customer nothing for the belt and installation and apologized for the inconvenience. I never received the belt from my supplier, so it apparently was forgotten.

The supplier that did deliver the belt asked for more business, which they did get. The original supplier had a salesperson that called on us every week. He would come in, show a current "special" he had, thank us for the business, then leave. I allowed this to go on for two months, so at this point he had called on the shop eight times. On week nine, I asked him if they had any type of reporting that shows our purchases. He actually had a report with him and pulled it out. He was astonished that his report read zero sales for the current month and the previous month. I explained the belt situation to which he replied he would get with the store manager. The next day I received a visit from the store manager, who was very apologetic. She stated there were some new employees and asked if I remember who I talked to. I answered that I talked to her, to which the conversation became silent on her part. Why did I not let her know, how can we fix this, were the next questions from her. I informed her that first, we provide great customer service, and I will not allow a supplier to cause me to provide anything less. I had never considered the supplier that saved the day for me but have since and I really like their service, so you are the one that drove me to your competition. She did not feel I was being fair so I asked how long it would have taken her to figure out we stopped buying. The only thing she could come up with was, I am not sure. This supplier opened the door for their competition and the competition capitalized.

SALESPERSON

- In my years in outside sales, I was interviewed one time on a first sales call. I have wondered why more shop owners do not emphasize the importance and privilege of a person calling on them. I want someone that is going to take my business serious. I want a commitment from the salespeople I deal with that my best interest is always at the forefront of their thoughts. This does not mean I get special treatment away from their company policies, it means I have someone that is the absolute best liaison between their company and my company.

- Tell me your background.
  - Is this person from the automotive field or are they trying a different career path?
  - How long do they stay with a job?
  - Is this person qualified in all of their companies' programs?
  - What type of training has this person had?
- How long have you been with this company?
  - What position did this person start at?
  - Does this person change positions on a regular basis or are they stable in a job?
- What are your personal goals within your company?
  - What is this person's career goals (how long do they plan on staying in the same position)?
- What is the longest length of time you have called on the same customer?
  - Have customers trusted them in the past or does this person stick around long enough to build a relationship?

You will be visited by many salespeople. People selling auto parts, uniforms, office supplies, insurance, air fresheners…any and everything. You must place a front-line person that can deal with these salespeople without offending them. You do not know when you may need a product that you were presented at a later date. You also do not have time to dedicate to every salesperson that enters your business. There needs to be a process to "get to you" and beyond the front counter. Do you allow salespeople into the shop area? If the answer is yes, you must choose which people get the "golden" ticket and who can conduct their business at the front counter. I do not say the golden ticket lightly; salespeople should have the goal of getting into the shop area, but it is a privilege that must be earned.

SHOP MANAGEMENT SYSTEM

A critical part of running your business is having a dependable and proven shop management system. There are many features, and you must decide which would enhance your business. Below are some common features you will want in a system with the ability to add on more. Ask your parts provider if they offer a system.

- POS system for completing estimates & invoices
  - Service writer friendly
  - Scheduler
  - OE TSB's
  - Labor guide
  - Wiring diagrams
  - Common causes feature
- Ability to set pricing matrix for parts & labor
- Multi User capability
- User-friendly built-in templates for reporting & responses

- Maintenance plans & reminder ability
- Vehicle history records
- VIN decoder / Mobile APP
  - Make it easy for your staff to record vehicle information without having a computer in from of them
- Catalog data which is easy to see between parts vendors
  - Beware of systems that only integrate to a single parts provider
- Payment Processing
- Marketing
  - Ability to send reminders and thank you messages to customers
  - Integrated e-mail system
  - Appointment reminders
  - Reviews
- Inventory Tracking
- Reporting
- Website Hosting
- Customer communication
  - Chat
  - E-mail
  - Text
  - Social Media
- Medium / Heavy Duty capability, if applicable

AUTO PARTS
OUTSIDE SALESPEOPLE

Have you ever wondered why most independent auto parts store salespeople are the owner? Plain and simple, the owner has all the "skin" in the game and feel they can talk business with their customers in a shorter amount of time than someone hired to do this. However, this can be achieved if you are not the owner. You must act with authority on any subject the customer brings up. In other words, you cannot say, "I will get with our credit department and have them call you." The buck stops with you! This takes a special type of person, so "just anyone" does not make a good salesperson! You must examine yourself BEFORE you take a sales position. There are several factors to consider.

- This is not an 8-5 job! In many cases there is just as much time researching and following up as making the actual sales call. If you are not willing to put in the time, not only will you fail, but you can also cause your customers to fail. If you take over a sales territory from a person that simply went through the motions, you will need to start by earning credibility from every customer. Sounds easy! Remember, you own every complaint, compliment, and opportunity the customer gives you. It is not the previous person that shoulders the blame...IT IS YOU!

- It is not a job for the weak! You must be strong enough to stand up for your company and for your customer. This goes the other way also. You must be strong enough to stand against your company and your customer when you know they are wrong. At the end of every day, you must be able to lay your head down and know you did everything possible to maintain your integrity while standing up for what is right and against what is wrong. BEWARE: If this is out of character for you to stand against opposition, yet you have a strong desire and learn to do so, do not become a narcissist. Remember, you are seeking doing right, not being right. Do yourself, your company, and your customers a favor. If you are not 100% committed, DO NOT TAKE THIS POSITION! The last thing this industry needs is another "flavor of the month" salesperson. The same goes if you are considering changing companies. Too often I have seen salespeople go into a shop and the first question they are asked is, "Who are you with this week?"

Narcissism is extreme self-involvement to the degree that

it makes a person ignore the needs of those around them. While everyone may show occasional narcissistic behavior, true narcissists frequently disregard others or their feelings. ...People who show signs of narcissism can often be very charming and charismatic.

In plain English, someone who thinks only of themselves and thinks higher than they should of themselves!

- Follow up. You must have a desire to help your customer and follow up on every single item the customer gives you, no matter how minor it is. Your customer may even forget about having asked you to look into that matter. This is your opportunity to impress the customer. You must want to help people with their expectation being...it is simply your job to take care of them! Customers will test you, so be ready. If I am the shop owner and you are my salesperson, I am going to give you something minor that will not have a negative impact on my business if you fail to deliver. It may be to check on an invoice, labor claim, returned part, etc. Something I can easily call the store and have taken care of. Trust is built from experience, if you cannot follow up on the smallest details, why would I give you something big?
- Internal relationships, an area that is far too often overlooked. You should know your store staff well enough that when they are accused of something you can defend them, because you know they would not do what was accused, otherwise you will just say, "Yeah, they're an idiot" and lose credibility for your entire company.

The store staff should know you just as well. When the store is asked if they have an outside sales representative, are they going to say they have the best or, "We do have one, and good luck with them!" Building this relationship is critical and you must make the first move. Ensure your store staff knows where you are going and what you are going to talk about, even if it is painful for the store. The worst thing you can do is deliver a negative surprise to your store.

- Determine who you are! Say, "I know who I am!" You do not know how you are going to respond to certain incidents until you deal with them in real life. There is a large population of salespeople that will fold like a cheap lawn chair when placed into an uncomfortable situation. Determine who you are and what expectations you place upon yourself. The first step would be to establish what type of salesperson you plan on being. I have included a few examples below.

  - **CAN KICKER:** A person that has a "canned" presentation for one particular product and dependent on the immediate sale. When the product changes, the overall presentation remains the same. It is as if there is a script that says, "Place product name here" when there is a change. If you like old television shows from the 1950s and '60s, these salespeople were everywhere. Selling vacuums one day, encyclopedias the next day and maybe toasters later. Today there are many in the automotive aftermarket. "I have a great deal on brake clean on this flyer." Thus, the name, can kicker. Imagine kicking a can down the street, you do not care what kind of can it is (soup can, bean can, oil can, etc.) you are going to kick them all the same. In other words, you are simply going through the daily motions. There is nothing wrong with selling something from a sales flyer…if that is the last thing you discuss after talking business.

- **CLOSER:** A person who is dead set on making a sale and willing to pay any cost for that sale. Beware if your company sells equipment, you could fall into this category, if you are not careful. This type of salesperson is constantly following up to close the sale. For the sake of not offending any segment of business, image yourself calling the customer every day and asking, "What do I need to do to get you to pull the trigger on the equipment I quoted you." Most importantly, these people have an "at all costs" attitude about making the sale and often damage a relationship by trying to make a singular sale.

- **RELATIONSHIP BY ENTERTAINMENT:** This is one of my favorites. I must tell the story of a salesperson that called on our repair facility. They worked for an independent auto parts provider and were good at what they did (according to him). This person always had a funny joke and was quite entertaining in the way the joke was told. This person could also tell you all the "dirt" on the shop down the street, which meant they would tell other shops any Intel they could get from our business. These people will say anything to make you like them. This was a nice person, always thanked us for the business before leaving. The issue was, we did not buy from this company…and the salesperson did not know this. This is a category that is very easy to fall in to. Be mindful, this is a hard person to trust and rarely do they have 100% entitlement from their customers.

- ○ **BUSINESS RELATIONSHIP:** In case you have not figured this out by now, this is where you want to fit. This person has an agenda before entering their customer's business. They always…always, follow up from their previous visit. This person will have things to mention to make the business better. This could be an upcoming training class, a program the customer could benefit from, or they have a strong enough relationship with the customer that they can tell them how bad the pothole is in the driveway, and this could be an issue for customers. This person studies their customer and knows the intimate details of the customer's business. They know the shop labor rate, the type of customer the shop has, the parts brands that are important to the shop…every detail. On top of this, they know who the shop owner's family is and what they are going through. What if your company had a scholarship program and your customer has a child entering a field the scholarship could help with? What if the shop owner's wife was going through a medical situation and you never mentioned or asked how she is doing? Doctor bills could be adding up and putting a strain on the business. Can you help? Only if you are aware! Americans became intrigued with investigation type reality shows, this salesperson performs their own investigation on every visit, and they do not need to survey the customer to get answers. Remember, trust is built on experience. It takes time to build a business relationship; the shop owner must know the extent to which you can be trusted.

I was discussing business with a vendor at one point in my career who was dependent on the immediate sale. My intent was to let the person know that anytime they worked with my company and my customers, the follow up required must happen. The vendor's reply was something I had never thought of; here it is: "We are hunters while your salespeople are farmers. We sell a product customers will most likely need one time, then we are on to the next hunt. You cultivate relationships where you do not make an instant sale every time while my company depends on the immediate, one-time sale. After the sale, we leave...for good."

You may have vendors you rely on to sell a product or systems that have this sales philosophy. You must know this and be willing to take up the slack when you are the one that presented and introduced this person or company to a customer and the customer needs follow up. You are the mediator and complete transparency is required. Tell the customer this representative is not coming back, if that is how they do business. However, if you purchased something represented by my company, I am your person for follow up. This could be a training provider, product representative and even a system representative. When you introduce a person or company to represent you, OWN IT! It is your customer you have been cultivating, building trust with, and communicating with on a regular basis. Vendors should know you well enough to understand your stance with your customers. It is as if you are a shepherd protecting sheep. "You want to visit my customer on my behalf? Make me understand what you are going to discuss and your philosophy. THEN, I will decide if I open the gate for you."

WE NEED EACH OTHER MORE THAN EVER

As our world has changed, the parts business has had retailers that never considered the wholesale side of the business that now do. These competitors are leading with price and shops are giving them business based on price alone. So, it has become very competitive to the point there are now internet sites that are giving even better prices. Remember, these internet stores are not invested in your community. They do not have a chain of physical locations and they are not people from this industry. The temptation is great to use one of these suppliers…until there is a problem and no one to turn to. While the shop is ordering their large items from the internet, the expectation is for the local supplier to be available for the small items and just in case the internet provider does not have the product they need. Seems unfair! I even had a shop ask for us to sponsor their baseball team as we had every year, yet they bought their parts from the internet. Why doesn't this internet supplier sponsor their baseball team?

Simple, they are not invested in the local community.

While this has been going on, there are internet sites that are advertising repairs for vehicles. You can input the job you are looking to have completed, your zip code, and the system will calculate the average cost to have this job completed at a local repair facility. Now, the repair shops are faced with selling against a system that does not care who they are and in fact, where they are. To add insult to this, there are now national mobile repair companies popping up where a van will show up at your location to perform repairs. They will come to your home, work, or wherever you desire. These companies have no investment in real estate and no interest in your community. They are simply making money on convenience.

This is important as our actual landscape, as we know it, could deteriorate. No local auto parts stores, no local repair facilities, etc. Suppliers and repair facilities must partner together and build a more attractive system than an internet company providing auto parts and a mobile mechanic completing the repairs. Between parts and repair, there should be groups meeting together and yes, this means you and your competition should join together to do this. Lobby with government officials in your area to make it difficult for companies to conduct virtual business as this places you at a very unfair advantage. You pay tax on what you purchase, either directly or through your customer. You pay property tax. You invest in real estate to conduct your business. This is a threat to your local government and community. If you are forced out of business by virtual companies, how will your community survive?

ARE MORE CHANGES COMING?

Understanding we cannot predict the future; history and reality tell us change is definite. Look at the masterpiece we call the automobile and the changes since it was first "invented". We should have learned that change happens every day, which should draw us to the conclusion...BE WILLING TO EAT CHANGE FOR BREAKFAST.

As I have reflected on my humble 40+ years in the automotive aftermarket business, one thing is for sure...change has happened. The winners have embraced change and ran away from the pack! So, what is next? The autonomous vehicle? Maybe, although Americans like having control of their lives and this seems to take the control away so it could be a hard sell.

For sure adaptive driving, which makes the roads safer. Your vehicle can check your tires, keep you in your lane and stop for you when you do not react fast enough.

Vehicles now have embedded cameras and so many shop owners are refusing to invest in the ability to reset these cameras. Imagine if you are in the windshield business and refuse to invest in this; you would be out of business.

The same is true for the automotive repair business. It is a good thing we cannot see around the corner to what is coming our way! You may ask why. Simply because, if we take our focus off what challenges we currently have and only look for tomorrow, we will lose sight of the business standing in our shops today.

REFLECTION

I hope you have gotten something from these writings and can put these thoughts with your own to develop a winning business! My intent is to have encouraged you in the automotive aftermarket; to look at the automotive aftermarket career as something that can sustain you and your family.

Enjoy people, enjoy life, and share your joy with others!

About the Author

Ron Todd grew up in Coweta, Oklahoma and began his automotive career in 1974 at the age of 14. His first job was a part time counterperson at an independent Green Light auto parts store. The owner of the store purchased a full service gas station in 1977. Ron would open the station at 5:30 A.M. and operate it until 7:15 A.M. then go to school. He would finish his day by running the auto parts store after school and closing it of an evening and working Saturday's at the auto parts store. After high school, Ron worked in an automotive aftermarket distribution center managing the customer service department for company owned and independent jobbers. Later, Ron became a district manager calling on independent jobbers. In the mid 1980s, Ron worked for an independent auto parts jobber, eventually buying the jobber store himself. In the early 1990s, Ron spent several years in his families automotive repair business later returning to the auto parts side. Ron has held positions in the auto parts business of store manager, area sales manager, regional manager, regional sales manager, divisional sales manager and director of professional customer sales. Ron has traveled the span of 34 states throughout his career in the automotive aftermarket spending the majority of his time inside automotive repair facilities either running them or selling auto parts and services to them.